"Somewhere in New England one will find Purgatory ᵣ Charles Coe with this region of America as much as I do W.E.B. Duꜱᴏᵢꜱ. In his latest collection there are many poems of mindfulness and daily rituals. Coe writes about aging as well as close encounters with white people that are lessons passed down from fathers to sons. His haiku are snapshots. There are lines in *Purgatory Road* that are as memorable as one's heart beat. "A squirrel is dragging a large slice of cheese pizza up a tree..." Lines like this will stop a reader somewhere between heaven and hell. Coe writes like a man with polished wings, flying above it all while watching the high and low tides of life."
— **E. Ethelbert Miller**, co-editor, *Poet Lore* magazine and founder/ director of the Ascension Poetry Reading Series

"In *Purgatory Road*, Charles Coe has given us a contemporary urban Spoon River Anthology. Empathy, fellow-feeling, Caritas, Metta, call it what you will, Coe brings his whole joyful heart and his considerable craft to the portrayal of both the living and the dead ("an endless parade of ghosts.") Time and again these poems not only remark on the distances between us but invite us to close them; they even sometimes suggest how. Coe speaks of — and with — a kind of neighborliness that moves from curiosity to attention, from puzzlement and mirth to warmth and appreciation. This is the work we need now."
— **Richard Hoffman**, author of *People Once Real*

"Charles Coe is a classic storyteller who crafts anecdotes, parables, and poems of fable-like quality—in a language as forthright as it is unfussy. Often beginning in the quotidian, Coe pitches us into greater realms, and through time's portals in striking ways. A number of *Purgatory Road's* poems are stamped with the author's inimitable wit; some bear the gift of the surprising journey. All, however, reflect his talent as a noteworthy raconteur."
— **Danielle Legros Georges**, author of *The Dear Remote Nearness of You*

Charles Coe

PURGATORY
ROAD

Charles Coe

PURGATORY
ROAD

Leapfrog Press
New York and London

Published in 2023 by
Leapfrog Press Inc.
www.leapfrogpress.com

Printed in the United States of America

Distributed in the United States by
Consortium Book Sales and Distribution
St. Paul, Minnesota 55114
www.cbsd.com

Back cover author photo © Gordon Webster
Image page 69 © Anne Nowselski 2023
Design and Typesetting: James Shannon

First Edition

ISBN: 978-1-948585-69-9

Table of Contents

I

II

III

I

Purgatory Road – Charles Coe

"I believe that what people call God is something in all of us. I believe that what Jesus and Mohammed and Buddha and all the rest said was right. It's just that the translations have gone wrong." – *John Lennon*

Some poems in this collection have appeared in *Ibbetson Street Press*, *Meat for Tea*, *Multiplicity Magazine*, and *The Red Letter*.

I

haiku for a new season

when will it be time
for all the ancient angers
to melt like spring snow

Opportunity

A woman in the park stands talking to a friend
while a little girl sitting behind her on a bench
feeds an ice cream cone to the family dog.

Dogs are noted opportunists where food is concerned,
and this one's no exception, making short work
of the job at hand (or rather, the job at tongue)
while the woman's attention is elsewhere.

Funny how our idea of what's important
changes with time. When I am older and grayer
looking back on this day, I won't remember
the headlines, the daily litany of atrocities and disasters.
I won't remember the comings and goings
of some flavor-of-the month celebrity.

I'll remember the way the wind tossed
dry leaves on a sunny autumn afternoon.
I'll remember a dog's tongue,
resolute and efficient,
and a little girl's conspiratorial smile.

Photograph

In those last months, those last days
before your dimming lamp
could no longer safe guide your way
you'd speak of shadowy figures
hiding in your yard behind the trees,
watching the house with binoculars.

In those last months, those last days,
you'd sometimes wear one sandal and one sneaker
or sit for hours with a book you could no longer read
clutched like a treasured but mysterious artifact
from some vanished world, and your husband
once found your missing gloves in the refrigerator.

Not long before you climbed into a car
for the ride to that place from which
you would not return, I stood in your kitchen
while you showed me a picture on the wall
of your two sons, now grown.

They were boys in the photo.
It was summertime, and they were at camp.
You said they'd been a little nervous, but excited
to go off without their parents. With a finger
that trembled only a little you pointed out details
with a wistful smile: the new tennis rackets,
the Red Sox caps, the lake in the background
that scared them at first
because they'd swum only in pools,
but they jumped in because they didn't want
the other boys to call them sissies.

I smiled as well, and nodded as you pointed
at a blank spot on the wall, at a photograph
that hung in some quiet corner of your mind.

One of These Things
Is Not Like the Other

A young man on the supermarket parking lot standing by a beat-up old Ford sedan with the hood up, glaring at the engine like he woke that morning thinking, "If one more fucking thing goes wrong today…"

And here it was. One more fucking thing.

A high-end Mercedes SUV was parked next to him and a middle-aged woman seemed to make a point of not looking his way as she tossed her bags inside and moseyed on down the road.

A parking space and a world apart.

Vortex

A pick-up truck pulls onto the mall parking lot
and the driver hops out and slams the door,
face set in anger, striding across the asphalt.
A young boy climbs slowly from the passenger side
runs after him, catches up and trailing behind,
head down says, "Daddy, you don't want me."

His father says nothing for a long moment,
finally mutters, "It's just that I get mad
when you do stupid stuff." He says nothing more,
never looks down at the boy now walking beside him
into a vortex that waits patiently to swallow them both.

Inquisition

What were you wearing?
Did you have a lot to drink that night?
Were you doing drugs?
Did you do or say something to lead him on?
Could you have misinterpreted his intentions?
Do you realize how an accusation like this could damage his career?

Do you have a problem with men?

Default Through Death

The summer before my freshman year in college I worked for a company that administrated federal college loans. I was in the "default through death" section, spending my time unstapling loan packages, filling in a form that listed cause of death, and in those days before recycling, dumping the rest into a giant trash barrel.

Car accidents, plane crashes, cancer and leukemia, drownings, murders, suicides...

a summer spent by the side of a road, watching an endless parade of ghosts.

Snapshots from Cuba

I
In Havana on a tourist bus, plush, comfortable seats,
air conditioning, a cooler in back filled with ice, bottled water,
and apple juice, snacks in a bag behind the driver's seat.

While we're stopped at a light next to a crowded city bus,
I meet the eyes of a man standing, hanging from a strap,
body sagging with the weight of a day's work,
rough clothes covered with dust and dirt.

We are separated by two layers of glass, and a slice of hot,
humid air, three feet and a million miles apart.

II
A young boy alone, kicking a soccer ball in a dirt yard,
two boxes against a fence for a makeshift goal,
moving to silent salsa.

III
Three men, two locals and a tourist, sharing a drink,
surrounded by cats wandering the plaza.
Tourist says, "When I was here in '92
I don't remember seeing so many cats."

The locals exchange a glance. One says,

"Well...things are better now..."

Scenes from a Vanished City

The teenaged boys who hung out in front
of the pinball arcade, smoking cigarette after cigarette
under the suspicious gaze of the cop on the beat.

The old black man in what's now a real estate office
who dished out ribs and fried chicken and collard greens
and mac and cheese to drunken revelers pouring
from parties and clubs at closing time.

The little storefront coffee houses,
where earnest young people sang and strummed
odes to the world they dreamed of creating.

The windows of skyscrapers that glowed
like burnished gold in the late afternoon light
as you passed in the elevated train.

The young black man in the ancient
heavy coat he wore in weather fair or
foul who sat on the steps of a boarded-up
brownstone, now a multi-million-dollar property,
and never spoke, just stared into a future
only he could see.

High Tide, Low Tide

As a land-locked child of the Midwest I learned in school that tides were caused by Earth's rotation and the gravitational pull of the moon. But I'd seen the ocean only in movies and on television, so that knowledge was an abstraction.

I'd lived on the East Coast for many years but the ocean wasn't part of my DNA. I once astonished a friend who'd been born and raised in a coastal town when I told her there'd been summers I'd never made it to the beach.

But then something happened. I spent a week in Gloucester, writing in a cottage on a bay where waves lap against the seawall under the porch. At high tide I could have hopped over the railing into the water. At low tide the flats stretch far away, and ducks and sea gulls poke their beaks into the mud in search of treats. I'd lean over the railing then to see what the receding waters left behind, ancient shells and skeletons, rocks strewn with seaweed, the occasional bottle tossed by some thoughtless human.

Being anchored in one spot so close to the water drew me into the rhythms of the tides, a ceremony ancient before people walked the earth, before dinosaurs, before meandering rivers carved the Grand Canyon. I started checking the tidal chart on the refrigerator. I watched moonlight sparkle on the water at high tide, and began to understand for the first time how those who grew up near the ocean never seem truly content away from it, never truly content away from this eternal dance between the Earth and her sister Moon.

I Wish I'd Held My Father's Hand

My father put what he wanted to buy on the drugstore counter and said a polite "Good Afternoon" to the young white clerk, who didn't return the greeting or meet his eye, just stared at the items as if Father had dumped a bucket of kitchen scraps, and then with exquisite slowness that dripped contempt, began to ring them up.

It was an ordinary day in Indiana in the early sixties. Everywhere a black man went he had to bite his tongue. Looking back over the years, I wish I could go back to that afternoon when my father stood quiet and still while that punk tried to put him in his place. I wish I could have caught his eye, delivered the silent message that I understood what he had to go through every day to keep the peace, to raise his family.

I wish I'd held my father's hand.

How to Walk Past White People on the Street

Some calculus is involved, and the ability to do rapid situational assessments.
On a busy sunlit city street serious analysis is seldom required.
You will pass each other without speaking or meeting eyes, as city people usually do.
At night when there's no one around, you might be the object of attention,
if not suspicion. It might be best then to avoid trying to make eye contact or offer a greeting.

The odds of being shot and killed by police, or a self-appointed vigilante while committing the crime of "Walking While Black" are actually fairly low.
More likely is that you'll get stink eye from someone who sees you somewhere they don't think you belong. Someone like the very old white man
exiting a luxury hotel as I was going in, who when our eyes met seemed to me longing for a better time when I'd be at the service entrance,
not walking through the front door, like an actual person,
to meet a friend for a drink at the bar.

Blocked

A young white woman in a high-end Mercedes coupe pulled up while I was standing on the sidewalk checking a phone message, honked her horn and glared at me. "Move it," she demanded, jabbing her finger at a car blocking her driveway.

I just shook my head. "Not my car."

She obviously wanted to say something else, but realized anything she came up with would have sounded idiotic, so she pulled over and got on her phone, presumably to get the offender towed.

As I passed I was tempted to say, "Be careful what you assume," but the last thing I needed was some bogus 9-1-1 call about a black man harassing a white woman, so I just headed on down the road.

You pick your battles...

Elegy

A dead baby deer is lying by the side of the highway,
a flash of white and brown I notice
in a fleeting moment of surprise and dismay.

We all have seen possums and squirrels
and raccoons and whatnot
killed on roads and highways,
but I have never seen a deer, and I'm
flooded with unanswerable questions:
did it wander away from its mother?
Was it orphaned and stumbled in confusion
onto this highway for its first and final
encounter with the world of humans?

Did someone pull onto the shoulder,
drag it to the side of road, take out
a phone and with shaking fingers
punch in the numbers to inform whatever
earthly authorities oversee such matters?

I speed along in my two-thousand-pound chunk
of metal, captured by the irrational thought
that there was something I might have done,
or could do now.

But I have nothing to offer, nothing to add.
Can only think of deep forests that will go
unexplored, and tender green leaves untasted.

II

Butt Dialing Jesus

There was a time when voices emanating from my pants
would have caused concern. But now I simply shrugged
and pulled out my phone to hear a recording:
"You have reached The Son of God.
I am currently speaking with another supplicant.
But please hold; your salvation is important to me."

This was followed by music.
I expected celestial choirs, or maybe an elevator-friendly
version of "My Sweet Lord," but was instead treated
to acoustic Delta blues guitar, interrupted after
a few minutes by the voice of Himself, greeting me
by name and asking how he could serve.

I was startled. Didn't expect to actually get through.
"Umm...what's the one true religion?" I asked,
flustered, just to have something to say.
"All of them," he replied. "None of them."

I was taken aback. "What? That's it?"
"That's it," he said. "Follow the Golden Rule.
Leave the campground cleaner than you found it.
Anything else? I have a lot of people on hold."
I had nothing, and mumbled my thanks.

He said "Go in Peace" and broke the connection.
I put down the phone and stared out the window.
The guy across the street was clearing snow
off his sidewalk. Never really liked that dude,
but I grabbed my shovel to go lend a hand.

Incantations

Late one night our family was driving home, Father at the wheel, Mother dozing beside him, head against the window, our enormous Ford station wagon humming along, a ship sailing the asphalt ocean. When "PT 109" as I think of it now wasn't full of tools, Father let my sister Carol and me pop down the back seat, spread a pile of blankets and stretch out, drifting off sometimes, lulled by the vibrations of road.

The radio was on and there was a sudden crackle and hum as the station Father had tuned in gave way to a disembodied voice reciting the results of high school football games from some far away state. The seemingly endless recitation of unfamiliar places took on a hypnotic quality, an incantation like the Latin words, meaningless to me, the priest spoke at Mass as I knelt on the altar in cassock and surplus, waiting my cue to pour water over his fingers and hand him a towel to dry them before he gave communion.

I didn't understand how this was happening. I didn't know that at night AM radio signals can travel hundreds of miles by reflecting off the ionosphere, bouncing back to Earth, and being picked up on radios impossibly far away. I didn't know this phenomenon, "skywave," it's called, happens only at night, because the ionosphere doesn't reflect radio waves when warmed by the sun.

I didn't know the science, it seemed to me we'd just slipped somehow through a portal to another universe. As that spectral voice droned on I lay in back of the station wagon, mesmerized by the endless stream of numbers that symbolized the joys and disappointments of young gladiators who'd fought their epic battles under the lights, before families and friends, on grass-covered fields, in little faraway towns I would never know.

yard sale buddha

calm and quiet gaze
unperturbed by bric-a-brac
savors summer breeze

on turning seventy

breakfast cereal
would once go "snap, crackle, pop"
now, bones sing that tune

I Will Not Turn the Furnace on in September

I will instead make a pile on the living room carpet
of unrealized dreams, disappointments, and broken promises,
set it alight, and warm my bones by the flames.

Massachusetts Bay Authority Employee Werner Herzog When Asked Why Red Line Trains Are Running Slow

"Because the Old Gods lie moldering in their lonely graves, while the grinning Lords of Chaos dance under blood-colored skies atop the smoking ruins of their new empire."

"Also, there is a disabled train at Park Street."

Inauguration Day, 2021

Like the World's Worst Party Guest
you finally stumble out the door
kicking a table over
in a final gesture of contempt
sending shrimp cocktail and Grandma's
beloved punch bowl crashing,
eggnog and crustaceans and shards
of hundred-year-old crystal spread
across the living room floor.

There is no accounting for the carnage in your wake.
Some of what you have taken will never be returned.
Some of what you have broken will never be fixed.

Yet we are still here, exhausted but resolved
to rebuild and reclaim, gathering ourselves
and rolling up our sleeves as the light of a new day
shines through our broken windows.

9/11

watchful red-tailed hawk
perched atop a nearby ledge
ponders clouds of dust

Ascent

A squirrel is dragging a large slice of cheese pizza up a tree,
and it's unclear which weighs more--the squirrel or the slice.

The slice is clamped in its teeth, and it climbs
maybe a foot, slips a bit, steadies itself by digging
claws into the bark, then resumes the ascent.
My admiration is great; I doubt if I'll ever undertake any task
with the same degree of dedication and resolve.

The odyssey ends when it lays the slice out
in the crook of a high branch and proceeds to feast.
No white-cloth, three-star human establishment
has ever had a more contented client
than this squirrel, dining in its canopy of green
beyond the reach of cats and dogs
and the sneakers of adolescent barbarians.

Capistrano

A man in a torn, dirty overcoat
paces the sidewalk
in front of the coffee shop
slowly, back and forth
head down, talking to himself.
He's here often. Sometimes
he'll come in, sit awhile
have a conversation with the air,
then hop up and wander back outside
to continue his vigil.

Why does this place of all places
call him? What draws him here
again and again and again
like the birds who return each year
to fill the California sky?

Thwarted

A man standing at the library check-out desk has a toddler, arms wrapped around his leg, who makes a break for the door, giggling, seized by some sudden urge for freedom. In a few loping strides the man snatches up the escapee, whose legs continue pumping for a moment before he relaxes, accepting fate.

For the time being he will continue to endure being told what to eat, when to sleep, what to wear.

But the day will come when there will be no arms to hold him back.

The day when it's finally time to see what lies beyond the open door.

Evasive Maneuvers

You did not know that a plastic container
of leftover pasta salad has sat in the back of my
refrigerator since the Harding administration.

You did not know that I have socks in my drawer
older than the beautiful young bank teller who,
at my advanced age, I regarded this morning
with attenuated lust.

Now that you know these things
have I slipped a rung or two
on your ladder of regard?

There are creatures in nature that
sometimes pretend to be some other thing
to catch prey, or to avoid becoming prey.

The four-eye butterflyfish has large circular "eyespots"
on its tail. Predators assume those spots are its real eyes,
and are confounded when they attack and the
would-be meal flees in the opposite direction.

We are often called upon to justify ourselves,
to prove our worth, to shove our untidy parts
into a junk drawer or a cluttered closet.

Maybe we could take a note from the butterfly fish,
hold our true selves close and dear
and when need be offer up some colorful
misdirection that leaves our would-be predators
with only a mouthful of bubbles.

Quality of Attention

I'm at the kitchen sink washing dishes
and see through the window a little brown
rabbit making its way through the yard next door
ears and nose twitching, alert for predators.

As quietly as possible I lift the screen for a better look
but the rabbit freezes at the faint sound,
suddenly no longer flesh and blood,
but a stone garden statue sitting under
a chrysanthemum bush.
After a vigilant moment during which
I'm silent and still, it starts to move again,
nibbling and poking through the grass.

I'm humbled by this creature's quality of attention.
When I *think* I'm concentrating,
my mind is actually a leaky garden hose:
(My nose itches. Am I ready for that meeting?
Who's frying onions?)

I rinse a plate and put it on the dish rack.
When I look up again the rabbit is gone.

Beasts of Burden

Item from the "Cape Ann Light and Gloucester Telegraph," March 8, 1873: *"A block of granite was hauled to the Rockport railroad station on Wednesday that required thirteen yoke of oxen to get it through the streets."*

Curious people line either side of the dusty road, mesmerized by the slow procession, oxen pulling a massive wagon that creaks and groans under its load, an ancient and eternal slab, formed when the world was young, that will outlast onlookers by a hundred generations.

It would be a foolish to think these animals understand their role in history, that they know their load will grace some grand edifice of the young republic. They are simply beasts of burden who pull when prodded, eat when fed.

But millennia ago, long before human masters with yokes and whips, their ancestors freely roamed the endless plains. Now at night, lying asleep in barns, do they ever stir at the touch of some distant memory, some timeless dream of fragrant, waving grass stretching beyond the horizon?

Fish Story

At the supermarket with dinner company coming,
in something of a hurry.

I'm standing at the fish counter while the person
ahead of me is in the middle of a private piscine
consultation, asking whether to choose this fish
or that fish or this fish for a particular dish,
inquiring into the provenance of the finalists,
asking for cooking advice

and I realize this errand will not be a quick one
after all, that I will indeed be standing at this
fish counter until, no beyond the end of time
when the human race has long since vanished,
a fading image on the retina of the universe
and the Earth itself but a lifeless cinder
drifting in eternal circles around the sun.

Purgatory Road

We were told in Parochial school that Purgatory was the place for souls not damned to Hell, but needing purification before ascending to Heaven, souls guilty of unconfessed venial, not mortal sins. There was fire and suffering in Purgatory, but just for awhile. How long a while was not explained. But we were told that if you died before you confessed your venial sins the chances would pretty good you'd wind up in Purgatory.

Purgatory wasn't like Hell where the damned burned for all eternity. As grade school kids, the concept of eternity was somewhat unclear. But one day Sister Helen explained eternity by telling us to imagine a solid brass globe, the size of the Earth. Once every thousand years, a dove flies by and brushes the globe with the tip of a wing. The time it would take that touch to wear the brass globe to nothing is just the first second of eternity. Sister Helen scanned our small, perplexed brown faces and nodded, confident her explanation had gotten her point across.

My main takeaway was that that even if Purgatory was a drag, it was better than Hell. At least you eventually got sprung. I thought of Purgatory as Heaven's Waiting Room, like the doctor's office, tables piled with ancient copies of "Reader's Digest" and "Life Magazine" and "Highlights for Children." Only with fire. Of course, I wasn't foolish enough to share any of these speculations with the nuns or priests. We weren't allowed to question matters of theology.

The rites and rituals of youth, the mysterious incantations in a secret and ancient language, the calm, inflexible certainties of the Baltimore Catechism, the dark and quiet confessional box, are all dust-covered relics in my mind's closet. But one time, driving through a small New England town I passed a sign for "Purgatory Road," and the name tossed me into the Wayback Machine, to when my life was ruled by pale faces draped in black, who spoke with great assurance in the voice of God on all matters spiritual.

I think now that maybe this earthbound life is itself something like a Purgatory Road, that navigating the potholes of our sorrows and disappointments, the roadblocks of fear and failure, the endless random acts of casual cruelty, is our own rite of purification, that crucible of cold fire through which we all must pass to become ourselves.

Memories of Lent

Ash Wednesday morning Mass,
and the pressure of Father Ryan's thumb
as he smeared a black smudge on my forehead.

The spooky purple shrouds that covered the Crucifix
and Stations of the Cross until Easter Sunday.

Frozen Fish Sticks

III

Love in the Time of Corona

(with apologies to Gabriel García Márquez)

In ancient Greece, men shook hands
as a demonstration of good faith
to show they weren't armed.
In these days of fever and fear
we keep our distance, resist
the timeless call of flesh to flesh.
But the time will come again
to take the stranger's hand
embrace a friend, share a kiss.
Until then our cries for human touch
are dispatches from separate
battlefields, tied to passenger pigeons
we release into the restless night.

Something on the Wind

A car waiting at the red light has a dog
with head stuck out the back window,
tongue hanging, snout twitching, beguiled
by some intriguing smell. The average dog nose
is a million times more sensitive than a human's,
a bloodhound's nose, a hundred million times.

This dog's a mutt, not a bloodhound,
genetic fruit salad, a United Nations of Dog,
but it has a fine nose, and appears
unconcerned about its lack of pedigree,
focused instead on whatever it's sniffing,
and it occurs to me there might not be
a more contented creature on the planet
than a dog with head stuck out a car window.

The light turns green, the dog moves on to new
olfactory adventures, and I wonder what it
smelled here, what it smelled that
I could never detect with this feeble
human nose, even if that nose
weren't covered by this mask I'm hoping
will protect me from something on the wind.

Communion: Spring, 2020

Do you remember those times we'd all meet
at some favorite restaurant? Stepping in
from the cold, breathing clouds of garlic,
shrugging off coats for the welcoming hugs?

We'd examine the menu with the care
of archeologists blowing dust off a
newly discovered Sanskrit tablet. And we'd sit
so close, touching sometimes, passing platters
back and forth, everyone yakking at once,
pausing to join in a ragged chorus of
"Happy Birthday" drifting over from a nearby table.

And finally, as our ravaged plates made
their way back to the kitchen, sometimes
we'd pose for a picture taken on someone's
phone by an indulgent server, arms
wrapped around each other, grinning
like high school kids at graduation.

Now those of us who live alone
search cookbooks and computers
for the dishes we make for one,
post pictures of our creations online,
not to brag, but to share communion
the only way we can.

For Elijah

This road I walk covers
my shoes with dust
that fills the still, hot air.
The memory of every step
I've taken these past days
echoes in my legs and back.
Far behind me is a place
I will never see again.
Above me, storm clouds
draw in, close and low,
and birds under these darkening skies
seem to sense the changing winds.

So I walk, with hunger and thirst as companions
toward destinations unknown.
I see a house, a bouquet of lights in the gloom,
and standing at the rough wooden door
pause before knocking, wondering if he who answers
will take one quick glance before turning me away.

Or will he stop to look at my sagging shoulders
and dust-covered shoes, take time to read
the story in my eyes, and say to the child
clinging to his leg, "We have a guest."

Marooned

An elderly woman is standing on a traffic island
in the middle of a busy street, not waiting to cross,
just shouting gibberish.

She's holding up a plastic supermarket shopping bag,
waving it like a talisman at the heedless river
of cars flowing by on either side of the island.

Sometimes this world crushes us beneath the wheels,
and sometimes it just ignores us as it speeds along.
Maybe the purpose of her lonely vigil
is simply to shout, "I am here. I exist."

Night Birds

A young woman lies in the moonlight
along the banks of a river whose name
she does not know, head resting on a coat
balled into a pillow, sleepless ears
taking in the sounds around her,
sighs and snores and quiet conversations,
an old man's tired, dry cough
blending with a baby's cry,
night birds whose calls remind
her of the home she left behind.

She lies in the dark, remembering a place
she knows she will never see again,
the village where she laughed and played as a child,
where now, men with automatic rifles
swarm the streets like stone-faced farmers
who sow only blood and tears.

Her body aches from a day riding atop
a north bound freight train, *El Tren de la Muerte*,
where those who lose their grip
tumble to earth, often to their death,
while the train, like some blind, mindless
animal, rumbles on.

But in spite of everything she has seen
she still believes in the power of prayer,
so she prays to remain invisible
to the men from the drug cartels
who sell those they kidnap
into forced labor and prostitution.

She prays for a home with a warm bed.
She prays that there is goodness still
to be found in this world,
that those she meets at the end
of this long journey will be generous and kind,

and in the moment before sleep comes at last
the night birds at the river's edge
add their songs to her prayer.

Under the Eucalyptus Tree

A young mother walking to the clinic
sits on a bench to rest in the shade
on this hot and dusty day. She has taken
off the sling in which she carries her young child
and laid it on the bench beside her.

Her child dozes fitfully, hot with the fever
her mother's special tea could not break,
and she wipes the sweat from his face
with a damp cloth.

When she began this journey
Mother had frowned and said,
"I do not trust the people in that place,
with their pills and their machines.
The old ways are best."

Mother and her husband had not wanted to hear
about the nurse who had come to their village
to speak of the clinic, had not wanted to hear
about the calm gaze and quiet, reassuring voice,
had simply stood a long moment in the doorway,
faces carved in stone, then turned
to disappear into the little house.

Now, finally, the young mother sees the clinic,
just a little way up the road.
She gathers her resolve, takes a deep breath
and rises from the bench.

Perhaps she whispers a short prayer of thanks
to the eucalyptus tree that granted her
this moment of rest and shade,
and perfumed the breeze
with hints of mint and honey.

Secret Chord (for Leonard Cohen)

They all thought this little shepherd boy was a fool to face Goliath.
In truth I thought something of the same myself, tossing and sweating
on my bed of straw the night before that fateful day, visited by visions
of the giant's sword, long as I was tall, cleaving enemies from shoulder
to waist with but a single blow.

When I made music for Saul, my King, to soothe his troubled soul,
it did not anger me that he so feared the giant he had me do battle in his
stead. It was not my place to judge, but simply play my harp to ease his mind.

He would send his servants away so it was just the two of us,
the sound of my harp echoing through that spacious, ornate, empty
room, while he stared into the distance at something only he could see.

Now so many years later as this crown sits heavy on my own head,
I feel the burden of the throne. We who would be the kings or queens
of our own realms seldom realize how difficult it truly is to rule oneself,
seldom realize how quickly the years fly, all the words said or left unsaid,
all the golden moments that each of us lets drift to earth,
until in the end, one can become a master of regret.

Saul, my King, what do I say to you now across this gulf of years?
Do I say,
"Offer up your sadness, your fear, your failures, your weakness, your
longings.
Offer them up, offer up this song of your true self, to the one
who accepts it without judgment?

Who can know, can ever know, what secret music flows
like precious blood through the chambers of the human heart?

Things White People
Have Said To Me

You're so well-spoken.
You don't seem like you were raised in a ghetto.
I'm impressed you can recite Shakespeare and Walt Whitman.
You have such a natural talent for writing.
Could you read some of your "angry" poems?

You're not like the others.

Just Another Day
(for Juneteenth)

On the first day of the New Year, 1863, on a Texas plantation, a man opens his eyes as sunlight streams through the windows of his little shack. The windows aren't really windows, just holes in the walls covered with tarpaper when the cold winds blow.

This man rises from his rough bed of hay, splashes water on his face, and eats a breakfast of cold fatback and cornbread. It's winter time, too early to harvest sugar cane, work the press that rolls stalks flat to extract the juice, the press that longs to crush careless fingers. It's too early to stir the giant iron pots that splash boiling cane juice on your skin. January is too early to plant, or pick, or haul, or bale cotton. Those hot and thankless days will come soon enough. Today's a day to build stalls in the master's stable.

When this man steps out of his shack into the morning light, his woman is already gone. Up at the big house, nursing the mistress's baby, and after that will churn butter, and after that will sit with needle and thread, to mend a rip in the master's shirt, and after that will kill and pluck and gut a chicken, and after that will haul in wood and stoke the stove, and after that will weed the garden, and after that will go outside to stir a cauldron of lye soap, and after that will once again nurse the baby while her mistress sits on the porch, in the shade, sipping cool tea and reading passages from her Bible.

On this first day of the New Year, two thousand miles to the north and east a tall, bearded white man sits at a desk, pauses a moment, as if awaiting guidance, dips his pen in ink, and writes the words, all persons held as slaves" within the rebellious states "are, and henceforward shall be free."

As his pen scratches slowly across the page, two thousand miles to the south and west, a man and a woman toil beneath the Texas sun. For them, it's just another day.

Two years later another bearded white man will sit astride his horse in Galveston and read General Orders No. 3: "The people of Texas are informed that, in accordance with a proclamation from the Executive of the United States, all slaves are free." Maybe the man and woman who built stalls in a stable and nursed their masters' baby on the day Abraham Lincoln wrote the Emancipation Proclamation are still alive when those words spread like wildfire through the state of Texas. Or maybe they are not.

However you pray, whether you put your hands together to speak Holy Words, lower your head for a moment of silence, or simply lift a glass, take a moment to remember those enslaved women and men who lived out their lives never knowing they were now free, no longer chattel, never knowing they were no longer merely beasts of burden, subject to the whims and whips of overseers.

Divergence

Many years ago on a soft summer night
an after-dinner stroll
through a quiet leafy neighborhood
past fine houses that breathed wealth and ease
when you stopped on the sidewalk
to look at a first-floor window that cast
a golden glow on the dark street.

There was painting on the wall
a geisha in a red kimono, and below
sitting on a table, a large vase covered
with black and red dragons.

"Wow," you said, moving closer
gesturing for me to follow
and when I hung back you turned
and said, "Come look."

"Nope," I said. "The last thing
I need is for some white people to see
a black man staring into their house."

You looked at me a long moment
as I stood on the sidewalk, unwilling
to walk into the yard, and I saw in your face
pale in the moonlight, the mixture
of annoyance and disbelief.

We'd met not long before, and this
had been our first evening together.

It was our last.

I wonder if now, after so many years,
wherever you are, if you ever think of me
if you ever look back on that moment
perhaps knowing now what you didn't
know then about the world, and feel
a touch of sadness and regret.

I wonder if you ever think about
the two kayaks that rowed along
together for just that little while
then drifted apart at a bend in the river.

Performance Art

Three African men are standing by their cabs in front of the supermarket, talking and waiting for passengers. There was freezing rain yesterday and one of the men is scraping what's left of the ice from his windshield. But he's not actually scraping, rather he's tapping at the ice with a lack of enthusiasm so vast it's mesmerizing, and I stop to watch.

It could easily be performance art, maybe titled, "Man for Whom New England Winter Has Lost its Charm." In the piece he leans over the windshield, tapping, tapping, tapping, inside a circle of red velvet ropes hanging from brass poles. His admirers, more numerous by the moment, stand respectfully outside the circle watching, while black-suited gentlemen in mirrored shades and ear buds discretely circumnavigate the crowd maintaining order.

The audience "ooohs" and "ahhs" at every movement, speculating to each other in whispers. ("What's the meaning, the message? Perhaps a symbolic statement on the futility of man's eternal struggle with the forces of nature?") There's a gasp of surprise and delight when his indifferent tapping actually dislodges a chunk of ice the size of a thumbnail.

But our artist never looks up, never acknowledges his audience. His eyes are focused not on ice and snow, but on something only he can see, perhaps a row of coconut trees, near the ocean's edge, fronds waving in the warm breeze, and far out to sea, almost at the horizon, village fishermen slowly rowing home under a cloudless sky.

Examination
(for Phillis Wheatley)

How strange the moment must have seemed
sitting before eighteen august gentlemen
under their coolly appraising gazes
fielding their questions about the Bible
and the classics, and waiting to be assessed.

They stared, but no one touched you
the way they touched you down on the docks
 the day you arrived in Boston as a child.
When they squeezed your arm, and opened your mouth
to check your teeth. When they calmly examined you,
the little girl whose true name
had been tossed over the ship's rail,
and now bobbed on the waves of that endless sea.

For the Africans on Slave Ships Who Committed Suicide By Jumping Overboard

You had to plan carefully, wait for the moment
when a deck hand or first mate's attention was elsewhere
before climbing quickly onto the railing
to dive into the dark waters.

Sometimes a few of you joined hands,
gazed into each other's eyes a moment before leaping.

After suicides ship's officers would mourn.
Each death reduced the journey's profit.

Some of you believed you would rise from the sea
find yourselves at home in your villages once again,
walking down the hills where you played as children,
toward the smell of roasting yams and the sound
of crowing roosters, loved ones celebrating your return
as the morning sun licked salt water from your ebony skin.

Flight, Interrupted

Late night at a subway station. I'm the only one getting off, no one's getting on, and I stand a long moment watching the train disappear down the tunnel.

A solitary pigeon has somehow managed to navigate three levels from the street down to the platform and is walking back and forth along the tiles, cooing, head bobbing. As I walk toward the escalator it flies up to the ceiling, spooked by my nearness, flutters along the solid barrier, and finding no path to familiar sky returns to pace the platform, a little farther down.

I make my way to the escalator looking for an employee to tell but there's nobody there, never anybody there at night anymore, and as I reach the street and step into the cool air my poet brain instantly chugs into motion, the machinery of metaphor rattles and cranks, hissing steam and spitting images as I consider the bird's plight. Maybe Freud would have said, this isn't a metaphor. It's pigeon. A living, breathing creature with a beating heart like mine, trapped in a place it neither belongs nor understands.

But the seed of a poem has already taken root. I'm already comparing the pigeon's dilemma to every creature constrained and bewildered by whatever invisible ceilings keep us from taking wing.

in the days to come

in the days to come
when i have gone
to wherever i am going
sometimes when you
walk along the shore
stop for a moment
bare toes in warm sand
gaze at the rainbow sky
and i'll be there
the salt spray
kissing your cheek

CHARLES COE

Charles Coe is the author of four books of poetry: *Purgatory Road, All Sins Forgiven: Poems for my Parents, Picnic on the Moon*, and *Memento Mori*, all published by Leapfrog Press. He is also the author of *Spin Cycles*, a novella published by Gemma Media. Charles was selected as a Boston Literary Light by the Associates of the Boston Public Library and is a former artist fellow at the St. Botolph Club in Boston. A short film by filmmaker Roberto Mighty, "Peach Pie," that was based on his poem, "Fortress", has been shown at film festivals nationwide. Another short film, "Charles Coe: Man of Letters," also by Roberto Mighty was named "Outstanding Documentary Short" at the 2020 Roxbury Film Festival. His poems have been set by composers Kitty Brazelton, Beth Denisch, Paul Frucht, and Robert Moran.

Charles was a 2017 artist-in-residence for the city of Boston, where he created an oral history project focused on residents of Mission Hill. He is poetry editor of "Multiplicity," an online literary journal published by Bay Path University in Longmeadow, Massachusetts, and associate editor of "About Place," an online literary journal published by Black Earth Institute.

Charles has served as poet-in-residence at Wheaton College, the Newton Public Schools, and at the Chautauqua Institution in New York State. He is an adjunct professor of English at Salve Regina University in Newport, Rhode Island, and Bay Path University, in Longmeadow, Massachusetts, where he teaches in both MFA programs. He serves on the Steering Committee of the Boston Chapter of The National Writers Union, a labor union for free-lance writers and editors. He is also on the Board of Directors of The New England Poetry Club and Revolutionary Spaces, Inc., the organization that manages and programs activities at Boston's Old South Meeting House and the Old State House, site of the Boston Massacre.

Poems

Memento
Mori

Charles
Coe

The Bells of the Basilica
(for Mission Hill Church)

When the bells of the Basilica toll the hour,
a river of sound flows down Tremont Street.

It flows over the donut shop,
the pizza parlors, the post office,
the hardware store.

It flows over the Asian woman
who sits waiting for the bus, her ancient,
wrinkled face the map of a world
to which she will never return.

It flows over teenaged girls
released from the bondage of school,
who chatter in Spanish like colorful,
land-locked birds.

It flows over the college man
who wanders into traffic
staring at his phone.

The bells of the Basilica
toll for believers and non believers alike,
for the loved and the lonely,
for those whose stories are just beginning,
and those whose stories are closer to the end,

The river of sound washes over
everyone and everything,
on the miracle of this most ordinary day.

all sins
forgiven
poems for
my parents
charles coe

St. Christopher

Catholic legend tells of a man of great size and strength who carried travelers across rivers on his shoulders. One day his passenger was a small child who grew heavier with every step. When they reached the other side the man, tired as no other passenger had ever tired him, asked "Who are you, who placed me in such peril? It felt as though I carried the whole world on my shoulders." The child replied, "You carried not only the world, but he who made it. I am Jesus Christ the King." For generations, Catholics have carried medals bearing an image of the man Christopher, patron saint of travelers.

Some years ago, while planning for the yearly Christmas trip home, I bought a St. Christopher medal for the dashboard of my father's station wagon but forgot to pack it. I'd meant to mail later, but forgot. Then late one night I got a call that he'd had a stroke. He recovered, but could no longer drive. The enormous brown station wagon sat for months in the driveway like a grounded PT boat, then was finally sold.

The medal meant for his dashboard now gathered dust on my bedroom dresser. Christmas came and went, twice more, and I never gave it to him. What would I say? Here, take this reminder of all the things you can no longer do? But one Christmas I decided finally to take it home, and the last day of my visit, as he sat in his easy chair watching TV, I said, "I have something for you." I told him about the medal, when I bought it and why I'd held on to it for so long.

He reached out and I handed him the medal. He held it under his reading lamp, turning it this way and that, and put it on the table, next to the TV remote. Then he looked up and deadpanned, "Well you know, I still travel from the living room to the kitchen."

PICNIC ON THE MOON

Praying in the Dark

When I was a child, God ate fish
on Fridays—spoke Latin
with an Irish brogue.

On the day
of my First Communion photograph
our small, brown faces smiled
at the count of three
and a great white light
blotted out the world.
(That photograph sits in a box
on a shelf in my mother's closet.)

The nuns spoke often of the
power of prayer; I prayed for snowstorms
so I could stay home from school.
When my prayers were answered
I'd press my nose against the glass
to watch those fat flakes
dance in the night.

We prayed the day
President Kennedy was shot.
From the corner of my eye
I watched Sister Edna's hands
wrapped around her rosary
her long, trembling fingers
the color of fish
that live on the ocean floor.

There are words from ancient ceremonies
I can still recite.
There is the remembered whiff of incense
and the sharp, smoky smell
of candles extinguished after mass.

There is the dim and distant sound of bells...

The nuns told us
God doesn't make mistakes;
all suffering is for the greater good—to teach
or to cleanse.

I try to remember that now
when I watch the news
or hear cries in the night
of those about to slip
beneath the waves.

CPSIA information can be obtained
at www.ICGtesting.com
Printed in the USA
JSHW082132060323
38532JS00006B/6